YOUR KNOWLEDGE HAS VALUE

- We will publish your bachelor's and master's thesis, essays and papers

- Your own eBook and book - sold worldwide in all relevant shops

- Earn money with each sale

Upload your text at www.GRIN.com and publish for free

Angelo Arcuri

Europe's response to the changing economic environment

GRIN Verlag

Bibliografische Information der Deutschen Nationalbibliothek:

Die Deutsche Bibliothek verzeichnet diese Publikation in der Deutschen National-
bibliografie; detaillierte bibliografische Daten sind im Internet über http://dnb.d-
nb.de/ abrufbar.

Imprint:

Copyright © 2014 GRIN Verlag GmbH
Druck und Bindung: Books on Demand GmbH, Norderstedt Germany
ISBN: 978-3-656-74813-7

This book at GRIN:

http://www.grin.com/en/e-book/280690/europe-s-response-to-the-changing-econo-
mic-environment

GRIN - Your knowledge has value

Der GRIN Verlag publiziert seit 1998 wissenschaftliche Arbeiten von Studenten, Hochschullehrern und anderen Akademikern als eBook und gedrucktes Buch. Die Verlagswebsite www.grin.com ist die ideale Plattform zur Veröffentlichung von Hausarbeiten, Abschlussarbeiten, wissenschaftlichen Aufsätzen, Dissertationen und Fachbüchern.

Visit us on the internet:

http://www.grin.com/

http://www.facebook.com/grincom

http://www.twitter.com/grin_com

Europe's response

to the changing economic environment

Angelo Arcuri

Abstract

This research paper attempts to explain how and to what extent the European economy has changed in response to major events occurred over the last two decades. The analysis draws upon Darwin's theory of evolution to clarify why the adaptation process to the new economic environment has not been uniform across the Old Continent and notably why some countries have performed better than others. From an evolutionary perspective, special attention is given to the Italian and German economies, as the competitive gap between them has greatly widened in recent years, raising serious concerns about the political and economic stability of the European Union. Investigating the reasons underlying these asymmetric results provides useful information about the characteristics that the new international economic environment has discarded through a process of natural selection and those which have proved to be successful by giving a competitive advantage in the "struggle for existence".

Keywords

Europe · Theory of Evolution · Globalisation · Euro · International Financial Crisis · Sovereign Debt Crisis

JEL Classification F15 · F62 · E2

Contents

1 Introduction

Biology and economics are closely related disciplines, as they share a large number of concepts and ideas, such as competition, scarce resources and equilibrium.

One of the most interesting and famous examples of cross-contamination between these sciences is Darwin's theory of evolution by natural selection. In his autobiography, the English scientist reveals that he drew inspiration from *An Essay on the Principle of Population* by Malthus, who argues the tendency of populations to grow faster than available resources and deems high mortality a necessary check to restore the balance between them. Several economists, in turn, have subsequently been influenced by Darwin's thinking. For instance, in *The Theory of the Leisure Class* published in 1899, the American economist Thorstein Bunde Veblen claims that upper classes engaged in economically useless practices of "conspicuous consumption and leisure" are doomed to disappear. Similarly, Darwin assumes that parasites exploiting their hosts excessively end up destroying themselves.

Darwin's theory of evolution still represents an important analysis tool in economics, because it helps to understand complex change processes and their effects.

This research analyses the European economy's evolution from a new perspective and explains why some EU countries have adapted better than others to the current international environment. Germany and Italy are used as case studies, because they have responded very differently to the major transformations observed over the last few years. Two obvious questions now arise: what are the reasons for these diverging performances? What features are essential to stay competitive in the new world scenario?

This paper aims to answer these questions through a brief analysis that goes beyond the traditional boundaries of economics to examine cultural and sociological factors.

2 Major transformations in the international economic environment

Over the last twenty years, major shifts have reshaped the global economic map and marked the beginning of a new historical period.

Complex dynamics and events, such as the globalisation of markets, the introduction of the Euro and the 2008 financial crisis, may be considered the main drivers of this transformation process, since they have emphasised each country's strengths and weaknesses and amplified the result.

Such changes have been widely discussed, but their interaction should be investigated in further detail, in order to understand how and to what extent it has impacted on Europe and contributed to the creation of a new environment.

The globalisation of markets may be primarily viewed as the rise of a new trade order, displaying an ever-increasing cooperation and interdependence among countries. Two main factors have driven this evolution: the first one is the liberalisation of trade, through the progressive removal or reduction of tariff and non-tariff barriers; the second one is technology, that has significantly improved transport and communication systems and made them accessible and affordable to the wider community. As a result, people are connected, both physically and virtually, like never before; they can exchange products and services and share any kind of information regardless of their location.

In order to adapt to the new environment, some companies have adopted strategies aimed at meeting local demand, thereby differentiating their offerings by country or region. Other companies have launched the same products or services worldwide, to benefit from current trends in consumer demand or to influence it.

Globalisation also means competing on a global scale and dealing with the problems and opportunities that go with it. Over the last two decades, emerging economies, such as India and China, have met this challenge by drawing on their strengths. Low cost labour has been and still is an important competitive advantage for these countries, but it is not the only one, as they compete fiercely with developed economies in a wide range of advanced industrial sectors, requiring modern infrastructures and a high level of expertise.

In assessing the impact of globalisation on Europe and its business system, both qualitative and quantitative research methods lead to partial and controversial outcomes. However, it is possible to identify some general trends through a brief analysis based on three key factors: industrial production, exports and imports. As for industrial production, several Western Europe's firms have offshored some activities, mainly low value-added productions, to developing countries, in order to leverage cost advantages.

This phenomenon has raised deep concerns in Europe about deindustrialisation, loss of employment and competitiveness. Some companies have rejected criticism by claiming that manufacturing offshore is necessary to stay competitive and there is no alternative. It would be unwise to take a positive or negative stance towards offshore manufacturing, given its various forms and implications. Nevertheless, it must be recognised that unskilled and labour-intensive processes carried out in emerging and developing countries are sometimes complementary to advanced tasks performed in Europe.

An opposite process, known as onshoring, has been observed in the last five years: numerous European firms have moved their manufacturing activities back home as a result of the lower cost competitiveness of emerging countries. Offshoring is not as convenient as before, because wages have risen fast in strategic offshore locations, like China, and higher oil prices have boosted transportation costs. In addition, the global financial crisis and the resulting economic downturn have deeply impacted consumer demand in Europe and led companies to review their business strategies: consumers consider their purchases much more carefully and seem to be very sensitive to the concepts of customisation and quick response. In order to meet these needs, some companies have decided to be closer to their customer base and hence manufacture in Europe. Another factor should be taken into account to understand this ongoing trend: some European countries, such as Italy, France and Germany, have an advanced expertise and well-established reputation in various industrial sectors (e.g. fashion, food and mechanical engineering). As a result, several products manufactured in these states are often considered to be high-end goods. Their perceived quality has proved to be attractive to an increasing number of consumers not only in Europe and other mature markets, but also in emerging countries, where the upper classes purchase such products to signal their social status and wealth.

Globalisation has had a positive impact on European exports, thus becoming a powerful growth driver for the Continent as a whole and particularly for export-oriented nations, like Germany. Emerging economies have hugely contributed to this expansion, as their GDP per capita growth has generated an increase in demand for European products and services. The global financial crisis has prompted European firms to focus even more on such markets and to identify China as a primary target. Indeed, the Asian giant has come out of the global financial crisis remarkably well, whereas Europe has experienced a deep and long-lasting recession resulting in a sharp drop in domestic demand. EU exports to China have dramatically increased in the past five years, to reach € 148 billion in 2013. Following this steady growth in exports, China is now the European Union's third largest export destination. It is also the biggest source of European imports, before Russia and the USA. China supplies a wide range of goods and services and it is likely to become market leader in advanced industrial sectors in the coming years given sizeable R & D investments. In general, it is expected to further strengthen its position in the world economy, though it has been growing at slower pace than before and some macroeconomic indicators raise some concern about its future prospects.

It is worth noting that the globalisation of markets has enabled a financial crisis begun in the United States to spread rapidly to the rest of the world and thus to become a global threat. As previously stated, this crisis, in turn, has significantly impacted the dynamics of international trade and triggered an economic recession unseen since the Great Depression.

The triggers of the crisis are well known: easy credit conditions in the USA led several people to take out loans and buy properties that they could not afford. In 2006, the number of defaults and foreclosures on subprime mortgages rose drastically and spread to the overall U.S. mortgage market. Banks, hedge funds and other financial operators all around the world that had invested in the U.S. housing market through subprime mortgage-backed securities[1] were hard hit.

The subsequent collapse of Lehman Brothers in 2008 sparked a chain reaction, that destabilised the world economy as a whole: stock markets suffered heavy losses, large financial institutions and businesses failed and consumers' wealth declined

---

[1] Mortgage-backed securities (MBS) are debt obligations that represent claims to the cash flows from pools of mortgage loans.

dramatically. In 2009, GDP slumped by 4.5% in the European Union, which entered a deep and long-running recession phase.

Indeed, most of Europe has displayed high unemployment rates, weak domestic demand and rising levels of public debt over the past five years. Fears of sovereign debt defaults have led international investors to demand higher interest rates from European states experiencing serious financial problems. Higher interest rates have made public debt harder to bear and prompted some countries, like Greece and Ireland, to ask for bailouts.

In response to the crisis, the EU authorities have taken a wide range of measures aimed at enhancing financial stability and fostering economic growth. They include: European Semester, Euro Plus Pact, Six Pack, Two Pack and Fiscal Compact. The European Semester is a new instrument for *ex ante* coordination of national economic policies. To implement such coordination, each year the European Commission analyses all member states' budgetary and economic plans and provides recommendations. The Euro Plus goes beyond the European Semester, as it commits the 23 signatory member states[2] to carry out a list of reforms designed to improve competitiveness and convergence. Another important step forward is the Six-Pack, a set of measures on economic governance, aimed at strengthening the Stability and Growth Pack (SGP) and preventing and correcting macroeconomic imbalances. The Two Pack complements the previous act, by improving budgetary coordination and economic and financial surveillance in the Euro area. Perhaps, the most famous and controversial piece of the EU macroeconomic architecture is the Treaty on Stability, Coordination and Governance in the Economic and Monetary Union, also known as the Fiscal Compact. The treaty, entered into force in 2013, aims to strengthen fiscal discipline through stricter rules for participating member states[3]: the annual structural government deficit cannot exceed 0.5% of nominal GDP[4] and the member states whose government debt is above 60% of GDP must reduce the excess of their debt ratio over this reference value at an average rate of one-twentieth per year as a benchmark.

---

[2] Eurozone states plus Denmark, Latvia, Lithuania, Poland, Bulgaria and Romania.

[3] The treaty was signed on 2nd March 2012 by all member states of the European Union at the time, except the United Kingdom and the Czech Republic.

[4] If government debt is significantly below 60% of GDP, structural deficit can reach at most 1% of GDP.

This regulatory framework is supported by the European Stability Mechanism (ESM), an organisation established in 2012[5] to give financial support to Euro area member states facing severe financing difficulties.

The overall EU macroeconomic policy is often blamed for bringing about harsh austerity and stifling growth. In order to comply with it, most EU countries have undoubtedly made exceptional efforts, by introducing tax increases and/or public spending cuts. These measures have had recessive effects on the economy, especially in the member states suffering from high levels of public debt and other structural problems. A rigorous budgetary policy is an essential tool to ensuring stability, but it may be harmful in times of crisis, if it does not allow for investments supporting economic recovery.

The persistent financial and economic difficulties affecting the Old Continent have called into question the whole architecture of the European Union and stimulated a lively debate about the Euro[6]. An increasing number of economists, politicians and the general public argue that the single currency has contributed to worsening the crisis. One of the most common arguments against the Euro is that applying a single monetary policy to nations at different stages of development creates imbalances, because it does not take into account country-specific problems and needs.

Since monetary policy is managed at a European level, the EU member states can no longer use it as an adjustment tool. Consequently, some countries (e.g. Greece) have been forced to deepen their budget deficit to soothe their difficulties.

In addition, the Euro remained quite strong during the sharpest phase of the crisis, when a weaker currency could help the European business system and foster economic recovery.

When the world economy showed the first signs of improvement, the single currency appreciated further against the U.S. Dollar, thereby affecting the competitiveness of European exports. In particular, the strength of the Euro had and still has a negative

---

[5] The ESM replaced two previous temporary EU funding programmes: the European Financial Stability Facility (EFSF) and the European Financial Stabilisation Mechanism (EFSM).

[6] The European single currency was introduced in 1999 and used only for accounting purposes until 2002, when it started circulating in physical form and replaced the national currencies.

impact on Southern Europe's goods, because they usually display low levels of R & D intensity and thus high price-sensitivity[7].

The supporters of the Euro point out that it has promoted economic and social integration among different countries, increased intra-EU trade and prevented worse consequences during the global crisis. Even though there are different opinions about the single currency's advantages/disadvantages, some limits of the European monetary architecture and policy are generally accepted: for instance, the European Central Bank cannot issue bonds (the so-called Eurobonds), that might serve as a shield against international speculation and thus protect vulnerable countries, such as Italy and Spain. Also, the ECB's priority has always been keeping inflation down, rather than encouraging economic growth.

In summary, each of the major changes occurred in the last twenty years has had a strong impact on the international economic environment and posed great challenges to the European Union: competing in a global market, that implies more risks and opportunities, new export destinations and competitors; facing rising government debts and speculative attacks; ensuring economic growth despite tighter fiscal and budgetary rules and lower credit availability.

---

[7] The demand for low-tech goods, such as textiles, food and wood products, is usually more sensitive to price than the demand for R & D intensive goods.

3 Italian and German economies: two distinct approaches to change

Germany is a leading export country, both in Europe and at a global level. It has further increased its position over the last few years, by enhancing its presence in emerging and developing markets. For example, in 2003 German exports to China amounted to 18 billion Euros; ten years later, they were 67 billion Euros (Fig. 1). This is equal to a share of 45% of total EU exports to the country (Fig. 2). Germany has managed to benefit from globalisation, because it has quickly grasped new trends in international trade and adapted its export strategies accordingly. Furthermore, its manufacturing system is focused on capital goods and high value-added consumer durables[8], which are not very price-sensitive and thus avoid competition with products of emerging markets.

Unlike most European countries, Germany has recovered quickly from the global economic and financial crisis: after a drop of 5.1% in 2009, GDP grew by 4% in 2010. Over the last four years, the German economy has continued to grow, albeit at a slower pace (Fig. 3).

In order to achieve these results, the country has invested significantly in R & D, thereby improving the competitiveness of its products and business system as a whole (Fig.4). Germany has also modernised its legislation through a comprehensive package of structural reforms. New labour market rules, known as Hartz reforms[9], may be considered a fundamental part of this renewal process. They have created new job opportunities, provided additional wage subsides, reorganised the Federal Employment Agency and sharply reduced the unemployment benefits for the long-term unemployed. As a result, the labour market has become more dynamic and flexible and employment rates have risen steadily.

The common currency has contributed to further strengthening Germany's position as a market leader. For example, there are no longer exchange rate fluctuations within the Eurozone since the introduction of the Euro. This factor has enabled the country to increase its exports to its EU partners and to gain a large trade surplus.

---

[8] Consumer durables are a category of consumer products manufactured for long-term use (typically more than three years). They include cars, home appliances, consumer electronics, etc.

[9] Four laws adopted and implemented in Germany between 2002 and 2005.

In contrast, Italy has not been able to meet the challenges of the new international context due to a number of reasons. First, part of the Italian manufacturing system is specialised in low value-added productions, traditionally characterised by intense price competition. As a consequence, the process of trade liberalisation has enabled low labour cost countries to take on a leadership role in these sectors and thereby driven several Italian firms out of the market.

The global recession has exacerbated the problems of the Italian business system: a weaker domestic demand and more difficult credit conditions have forced a huge number of companies to close down or downsize, with a devastating impact on the economy and society. Small companies, which represent more than 90% of businesses in Italy, have been hit particularly hard in terms of revenue, investment and employment.

Unlike Germany and other EU partners, the country has not succeeded in overcoming the crisis: economy recovered slightly in 2010-2011, but decreased again in 2012-2013. The overall losses recorded since the beginning of the crisis are staggering: GDP dropped by 8.9% from 2008 to 2013 (Fig. 3).

These negative performances are rooted in structural weaknesses affecting both the private and public sector. As for the first point, Italy suffers from the so-called business dwarfism, since the majority of Italian companies are small-sized. This is certainly a disadvantage in a global economy, because small companies have to compete with firms with access to significant financial, technical and human resources. A closely related problem is a very low level of private R & D spending, that is widening the competitive gap between Italian companies and their foreign rivals.

The public sector and its inefficiencies are deemed to be responsible to a large extent for the current decline. In particular, one of the biggest threats to Italy is its public debt, which is one of the largest in the world at over 2 trillion Euros. This level of debt does not allow for significant tax cuts, which would stimulate entrepreneurship and boost consumption. Tax cuts have recently been introduced for lower-income workers[10], but a wider fiscal reform is needed and requires a systematic spending review. Another major problem is a heavy bureaucracy, that increases the cost of

---

[10] In 2014, the Italian government reduced taxes by 80 Euros per month for workers earning between 8,000 and 26,000 Euros a year.

doing business, discourages foreign direct investment and ultimately results in a loss of competitiveness for the country as a whole.

These structural points of weakness and especially the rising level of public debt have led financial operators to view Italian bonds as a risky investment. In November 2011, international market pressures on Italy rose dramatically, due to growing fears over a possible spread of the Greek debt crisis to other heavily indebted countries. As a result, Italy's ten-year bonds yield crossed the 7% threshold, considered to be a point of no return. The Italian authorities and the European Central Bank were able to reassure investors through an effective set of measures, which resulted in bond yields declining rapidly. However, the high level of public debt in Italy and other EU countries is still a threat to the economic stability of the European Union and even to the survival of the single currency.

On the one hand, the Euro has offered remarkable advantages to Italy over the previous situation, such as: better borrowing conditions, higher price stability, easier intra-EU trade. On the other hand, the common currency has deprived Italy and the other Eurozone's members of any control over monetary policy. For instance, the country can no longer resort to devaluation to boost its exports.

It is worth noting that Italy was much more competitive before all the changes analysed in this paper occurred. From a Darwinian perspective, the country was well suited to the previous environment, to such an extent that it was the world's fifth largest economy in 1987. During that time, Italian firms were not in competition with those of emerging powers; the government could stimulate economy through public spending without the current EU budget restrictions; the Bank of Italy could manage the monetary policy and devalue the national currency to correct payment imbalances.

Italy has lost its competitiveness over the last two decades simply because it has failed to adapt to the new environmental conditions. Similar dynamics may be observed in biology: those species that adapt to the changing environment can survive, while those which do not adapt become extinct. To quote Darwin: "it is not the strongest species that survive, nor the most intelligent, but the ones most responsive to change".

Italy's structural problems and economic policies seem to be the outcome of cultural and sociological traits. For example, the complex body of rules and regulations that makes Italian public administration expensive and ineffective originates from a culture of bureaucracy deep-rooted in all Latin countries. This explains why hyper-regulation remains a serious issue in Italy, despite several attempts to modernise and simplify the public sector. Yet, a certain degree of social tolerance towards behaviours pursuing particular interests at the expense of the state may be viewed as a crucial factor for the rise of public debt and tax evasion over the past decades.

The question then arises: what are the traits with "heritable variations"[11] that have conferred a competitive advantage to Germany and enabled it to succeed in the "struggle for existence"? The country's global approach to economics may be deemed to be the main reason for its success. A number of cultural, historical and sociological elements have shaped this approach. In this respect, it is worth mentioning the influence of Ordoliberalism[12], an economic theory which states that governments should ensure a healthy level of competition and thus prevent cartels and monopolies, but they should not intervene in the normal course of the economy. As a result, they should not adopt expansionary fiscal and monetary measures to foster growth in a recession phase.

Ordoliberalist principles and rules have had and still have a strong impact on Germany's economic policies and help to explain why the country has been able to keep public spending and debt under control.

Whereas Italy and other European states have only exploited their existing competitive advantages, Germany has also managed to create new ones, through significant investment in R & D and comprehensive strategies designed to gain a leadership position in emerging and developing markets. This dual focus in exploitation and exploration is an essential part of Germany's approach and the reason why the country is competitive in the current environment as much as the previous one.

---

[11] Darwin describes variation as "a feature of natural populations". Natural selection acts on traits having heritable variations and giving a competitive advantage in the struggle for resources.

[12] Ordoliberal theory was developed between 1930 and 1950 by German economists, such as Franz Bohm, Leonhard Miksch, Walter Eucken and Hans Grossmann-Doerth. It emphasises more than other liberal theories the importance of preventing cartels and monopolies.

4 Conclusions

Macroeconomic data suggest that Germany has been able to adapt to the new international economic environment better than Italy. A wide range of cultural, historical and sociological factors have led these two countries to make different strategic choices and thus to follow distinct evolutionary paths. Since European economies are deeply connected, Italy's adaptation problems should not be viewed as a mere national issue, but rather a serious threat to the whole European Union.

Germany is directly threatened by the economic and financial difficulties affecting Italy and other European countries, because these states represent a fundamental export destination for German firms and are essential to the survival of the single currency, which has largely contributed to Germany's recent expansion.

Despite its present difficulties, Italy displays a number of strengths, such as a primary budget surplus, relatively low levels of household and business debt and a vast manufacturing sector (Italy is the second largest manufacturing economy in Europe). If the country exploits its strengths and carries out a wide reform plan, it can fill the gap with other developed economies. Since the global financial crisis, Italian governments have introduced structural reforms in crucial sectors and several firms have reviewed their business strategies: for example, an increasing number of fashion manufacturers have moved to high-end and medium-to-high-end market segments to benefit from larger profit margins and avoid competition with emerging and developing countries. These changes show greater awareness of the new international environment, but must be followed by further efforts. In particular, because Italy's downturn is partly due to cultural factors, the first step to take is a radical education reform based on merit and innovation. Such a change would trigger a virtuous cycle benefiting all economic sectors in the long term. Nevertheless, all single countries' interventions are likely to be unsuccessful without the support of the European Union, which should play a more active role in promoting a closer integration among its members and place more emphasis on growth.

Acknowledgements

The author gratefully acknowledges the helpful comments and suggestions provided by Sarah Horne.

References

COUNCIL OF THE EUROPEAN UNION. (2012) Factsheet-Treaty Establishing the European Stability Mechanism. [Online] Available from: http://www.consilium.europa.eu/uedocs/cms_data/docs/pressdata/en/ecofin/127 788.pdf. [Accessed: 11th August 2014].

DARWIN, C. (1959) On the Origin of Species by Means of Natural Selection, or, the Preservation of Favoured Races in the Struggle for Life. London: J. Murray.

DULLIEN, S., GUEROT, U. (2012) The Long Shadow of Ordoliberalism: Germany's Approach to the Euro Crisis, European Council on Foreign Relations. [Online] Available from: http://www.ecfr.eu/content/entry/the_long_shadow_of_ordoliberalism_germanys_approach_to_the_euro_crisis.[Accessed: 18th August 2014].

ERBER, G., HAGEMANN, H. (2013) Growth and Investment Dynamics in Germany After the Global Financial Crisis. DIW Economic Bulletin. [Online] (2). p.15-24. Available from: http://www.diw.de/documents/publikationen/73/diw_01.c.415240.de/diw_econ_b ull_2013-02-3.pdf. [Accessed: 12th August 2014].

EUROPEAN COMMISSION. (2014) Facts and Figures on EU-China Trade. [Online] Available from: http://trade.ec.europa.eu/doclib/docs/2009/september/ tradoc_144591.pdf. [Accessed: 11th August 2014].

EUROSTAT. (2014) Real GDP growth rate – volume [Online]. Available from: http://epp.eurostat.ec.europa.eu/tgm/table.do?tab=table&init=1&plugin=1&langu age=en&pcode=tec00115. [Accessed: 19th August 2014].

EUROSTAT.(2014) Germany, Trade in goods with China [Online]. Available from: http://epp.eurostat.ec.europa.eu/portal/page/portal/statistics/search_database. [Accessed: 19th August 2014].

KREBS, T., SCHEFFEL, M. (2013) Macroeconomic Evaluation of Labour Market Reform in Germany. [Online] IMF Working Paper. International Monetary Fund. Available from: https://www.imf.org/external/pubs/ft/wp/2013/wp1342.pdf. [Accessed: 19th August 2014].

LECHNER, F. J., BOLI, J. (2011) The Globalization Reader. Oxford: Wiley Blackwell.

LEVITT, T. (1983) The Globalization of Markets. Harvard Business Review. 61 (5/6) p 92-102.

MALTHUS, T. R. (1992) An Essay on the Principle of Population (Cambridge Texts in the History of Political Thought). Cambridge: Cambridge University Press.

PISANI- FERRI, J. (2014) The Euro Crisis and its Aftermath. New York: Oxford University Press.

SALONER, G., SHEPARD, A. and PODOLNY, J. (2005) Strategic Management. New York: John Wiley & Sons.

VEBLEN, T. (2007) The Theory of the Leisure Class. Teddington: The Echo Library.

WORLD BANK (2014) Research and Development Expenditure (% GDP) [Online]. Available from: http://data.worldbank.org/indicator/GB.XPD.RSDV.GD.ZS. [Accessed: 19th August 2014].

Appendix

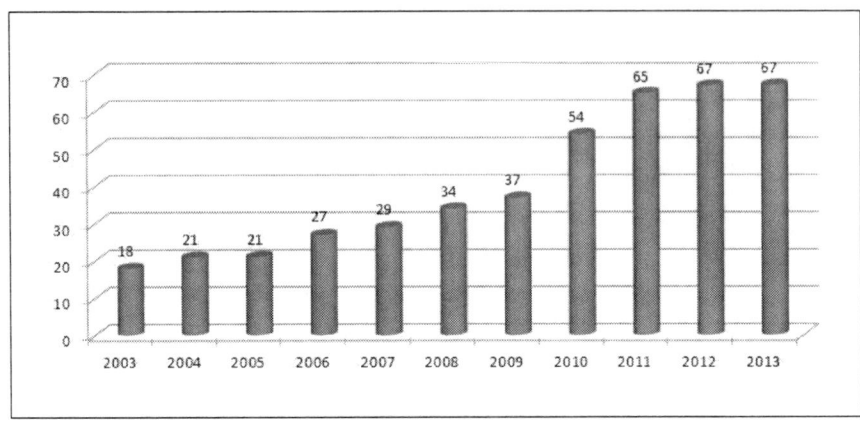

Figure 1 Germany's exports to China (€ Bn). Source: author's elaboration on Eurostat data - online statistical database

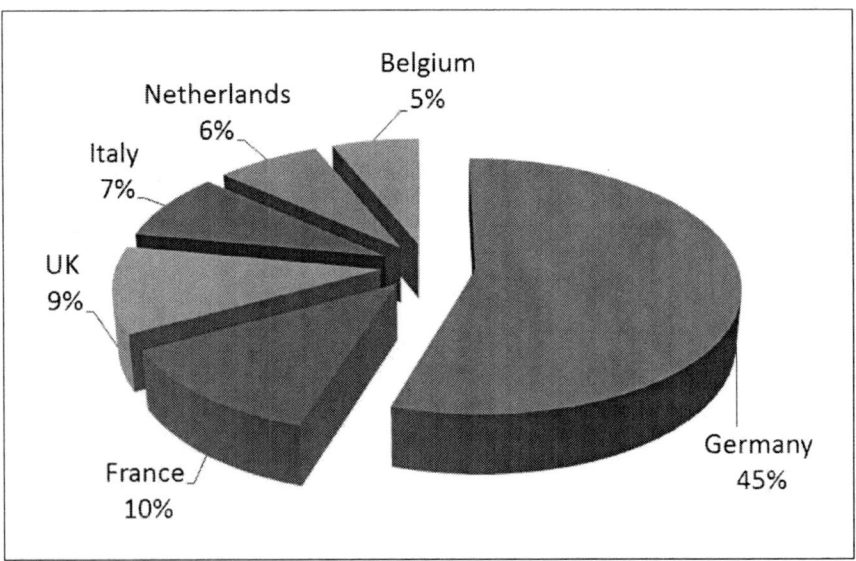

Figure 2 European Union's exports to China by country % Jan - Dec 2013. Source: author's elaboration on Eurostat data - online statistical database

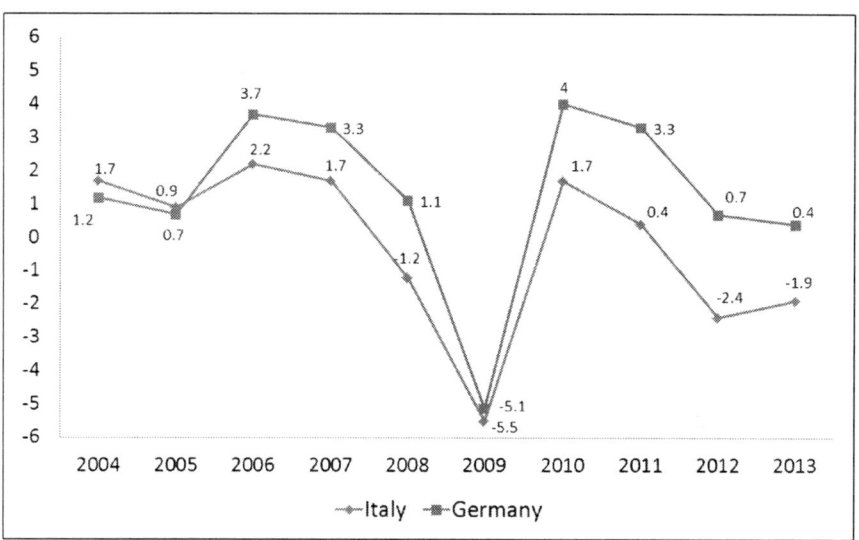

Figure 3 Italy and Germany - Real GDP growth %. Source: author's elaboration on Eurostat data - online statistical database

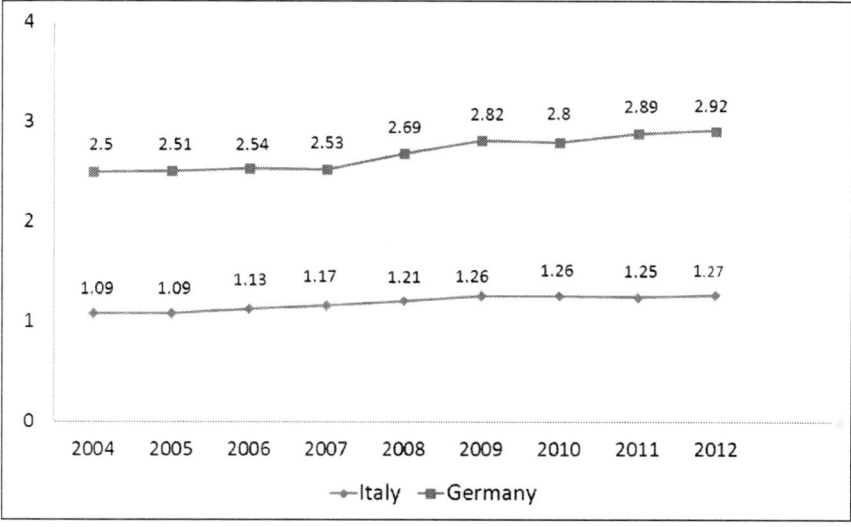

Figure 4 Italy and Germany. Research and development expenditure (% of GDP). Source: author's elaboration on World Bank data - research and development expenditure (%GDP) Tables

CPSIA information can be obtained at www.ICGtesting.com
Printed in the USA
BVOW05s0927021014

369225BV00004B/136/P